DO YOU KNOW
I LOVE YOUR BOW?

WRITTEN BY MANDIE WILDER
ILLUSTRATED BY ANNMARIE WEDIN

FOR MY THREE CHILDREN WHO UNKNOWINGLY GAVE ME THE COURAGE
TO WRITE THIS BOOK. I LOVE YOU ALL DEARLY.

I REALLY LOVE YOUR BOW; SO PRETTY
AND SO PINK. IT'S ONE OF MY FAVORITES
I REALLY TRULY THINK.

I REALLY LOVE YOUR HIJAB (HI-JAB)! IT'S SO STRIKING AND SO NEAT. YOUR STYLE MY FRIEND, DOESN'T MISS A BEAT!

I REALLY LOVE YOUR BINDI (BIN-DI); THE COLOR IS SO BOLD! IT SHOWS BEAUTY AND CULTURE THAT NEVER GETS OLD.

I REALLY LOVE YOUR BEADS AND BRAIDS- OH WOW, THEY ARE SO GREAT! I'M SURE SOME TIME AND LOVE WENT INTO THESE TO CREATE.

I REALLY LOVE YOUR BRACES, FRIEND. THEY MAKE ME WANT TO SMILE. HOW FUN TO PICK DIFFERENT COLORS TO MATCH YOUR AWESOME STYLE!

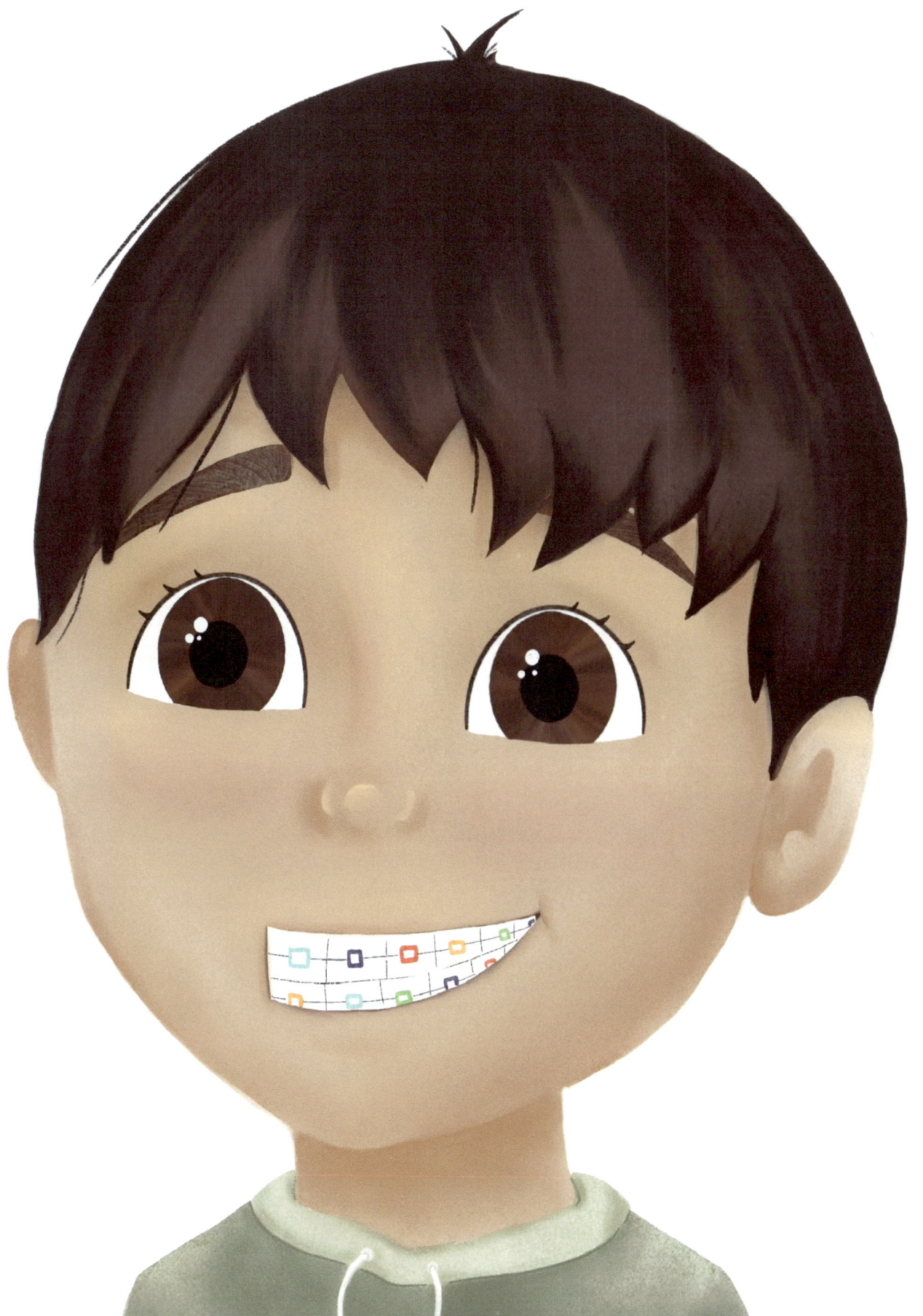

I REALLY LOVE YOUR GLASSES; THEY ARE SO VERY COOL! I BET THEY HELP YOU SEE MUCH BETTER AND PARTICIPATE IN SCHOOL!

I REALLY LOVE YOUR BEADED HEADBAND! HOW COLORFUL IT IS! THE DETAIL AND THE PATTERNS ARE SUPER FABULOUS!

I REALLY LOVE YOUR WHEELCHAIR! IT'S MADE PERFECTLY FOR YOU. YOUR WAY OF TRANSPORTATION LOOKS PRETTY COOL!

I REALLY LOVE YoUR KIPPAH (KIP-PAH)! IT Looks QUITE NICE I MUST SAY. IT REPRESENTS A PIECE oF YoU IN A REALLY SPECIAL WAY!

LOOK AT ALL OF THESE SMILING FRIENDS, WITH STYLES AND STORIES THAT NEVER END; OUR VERY OWN UNIQUE BLEND, THAT FILLS OUR LIVES WITH SO MUCH TO LEARN. IT ALL CAN START WITH ONE KIND WORD, OR CONVERSATION, OR SHARING A SEAT; MEETING NEW PEOPLE IS SUCH A TREAT!

DISCUSSION QUESTIONS

- WHAT IS A COMPLIMENT?
- HOW DO YOU FEEL WHEN SOMEONE COMPLIMENTS YOU?
- HOW OFTEN DO YOU COMPLIMENT PEOPLE?
- WHO DID YOU COMPLIMENT TODAY?
- WHO WILL YOU COMPLIMENT TODAY?
- HOW DOES COMPLIMENTING SPREAD KINDNESS?
- CAN YOU COMPLIMENT SOMEONE YOU DON'T KNOW?
- HOW DOES IT MAKE YOU FEEL WHEN YOU COMPLIMENT SOMEONE?
- HAVE YOU EVER THOUGHT SOMETHING NICE ABOUT SOMEONE BUT WERE AFRAID TO SAY IT OUT LOUD?
- WHAT WOULD HAPPEN IF YOU DID SAY IT OUT LOUD?

Find FREE kid-friendly supplemental resources for ages pre-k through 3rd grade (ages 3 years to 10 years) at courageousdahlia.com.

REMEMBER, IT CAN TAKE COURAGE TO COMPLIMENT SOMEONE, ESPECIALLY IF YOU DON'T KNOW THEM. THE GOOD THING IS, WE ALL HAVE COURAGE, AND YOU CAN USE IT!

COURAGEOUS MISSION FOR YOU: COMPLIMENT ONE PERSON TODAY WHO YOU KNOW, AND ONE PERSON WHO YOU DON'T KNOW.

USE YOUR COURAGE TO SPREAD KINDNESS.